"The practice of democracy is not
passed down through the gene pool.
It must be taught and learned anew
by each generation of citizens."

–Sandra Day O'Connor, *Supreme Court Justice*

Democracy for Dinosaurs
A Guide for Young Citizens

Written by
Laurie Krasny Brown

Illustrated by
Marc Brown

L B
Little, Brown and Company
New York Boston

Contents

Introduction

There you are, with your very own body, feelings, and ideas.

There's your family who helps take care of you.

Outside your family, you are part of your neighborhood, your school, the place you may pray, your play group, your club or team, a community center. But that's not all. You also are part of something much bigger: your country. Whether you were born here or moved here, now you live in America.

That usually makes you a kid citizen! Even babies can be tiny citizens.

What does it mean to be a kid citizen in America? What do you do?

Share Equal Rights

Sharing is a way of including others and not keeping things all for yourself. You've shared plenty of times since you were little. You hope people will share with you, too.

You probably know how it feels to be left out or included. Inviting kids into your game is also sharing.

Let's make some room here. Want to play with us?

Showing friends how your family lives is also sharing.

You may get to try out the way kids do things at their homes, too.

Sharing also takes place in a country. When no one gets left out, then everyone has equal rights. That means all citizens would have the same chance to share what America has to offer:

to feel safe,
to have a home and enough to eat,
to have clean water,
to go to school or have a job.

These are goals our government set when it began. Americans are still at work making these happen for everybody.

Kid citizens can help by sharing! Everyone has something they can share: their stuff, their schoolwork, their language, and their ideas.

What's this word? How do you say it?

Easy, that's *la casa*. It's *house*.

You are being a kid citizen who believes in equal rights when you treat everyone with kindness and respect. Try to look out for *all* your neighbors.

I really like your scarf.

Oh, thanks! It's my hijab.

Does everyone have pizza?

Considering others besides yourself adds to the common good—the good of all!

Yes!

Thanks!

Be Fair

Being fair is a way of showing respect, like when your teacher calls on each kid in class instead of just a few. Keeping others from being a part of something for no good reason is unfair to them.

Good rules help make fairness possible. If the rule is that everyone who signs up gets to play, then following that rule makes it fair for all the kids who want to play. Follow rules that benefit everyone.

It isn't always easy to be fair. How can you be fair to someone when you're mad at them?

Hint: Try calming down first. Take a bike ride or read a story. Or maybe count to fifty.

Okay, okay, she might be right.

It isn't always easy to follow rules, either. But every day brings a chance to practice!

Our country has rules, too, called laws. Laws tell citizens and the government what they can and cannot do. Attending school every day is following the law!

When the laws are fair to everyone, there is justice. Making justice happen in America is something we keep working on. As a kid citizen, you can help.

When someone breaks the law, we judge by what a person did wrong, not by who did it.

Except if the one ignoring the law is a baby!

In America, no one is supposed to be punished until there's enough proof they did something wrong.

If someone is responsible for what went wrong, the consequence needs to be fair. Rules aren't always fair, though. Not all laws are good ones. The goal in America is to keep making better, fairer laws.

Vote

Voting is a way to choose. As a kid citizen, you are learning to vote when you share opinions about what you like and don't like.

You can vote in favor of something. Or against something.

Make sure you vote whenever you can. If a decision is made without you, there is less justice. Your vote matters! Maybe your class needs to choose someone to be in charge of cleanup at the end of the day. You could hold an election.

Hold an Election

People who want a certain job are called candidates. If you are a candidate, try to convince the rest of the class, the voters, to choose you.

If you are a voter, how do you know whom to vote for? To be a smart voter, find out about each candidate, listen to what they say, and watch what they do. Who would be good at this job?

What if your friend is a candidate? Do you have to vote for her?

Make up your own mind when you vote.

What if the winner isn't whom you voted for? Let's hope she does a great job. If not, you have another chance to choose in the next election.

Messy Maria won.

Maybe she'll do a good job.

In America, it is up to citizens to choose who will lead the country. Once you turn eighteen and register to vote, you become an official voter!

The power will be yours to help elect leaders who can make better laws and decisions for everyone.

Be Honest

As a kid citizen, you are expected to be honest and tell the truth, with your family, your friends, and your teachers.

You mean what you say if you are truthful.

I can help you build a tower.

If you say you'll do something but then do something totally different, that's a lie.

Keeping a promise is another way to show that you can be trusted.

Being honest isn't always easy. It takes courage sometimes.

Sometimes the truth is right in front of your eyes, like an object that exists (the moon) or an event that happened (bedtime). It's a fact.

I have a baby sister. No doubt about it!

The truth can also be something you don't see, but it's agreed to be the way things are.

He's my best friend.

Yep, we're best friends, all right.

The truth is not the same as a wish, which may or may not come true.

I wish you didn't have to stay in bed and could play in the game tomorrow.

The truth is not the same as make believe.
Pretending doesn't make something true,
no matter how hard you try.

The truth is not the same as an opinion.

People aren't always honest about what is fake or false, and what is true.
It's important to learn how to recognize the truth.

Look for Truth

A kid citizen is always on the lookout for what is true, honest, and accurate. Sometimes the information you're given isn't always correct, up to date, or the whole story.

Here are a few tips:

Know **who** is telling you something. What is their source, or where the information comes from?

Understand **why** someone is telling you something. Someone may try to convince you something is true even when it isn't. Maybe they want to sell you something.

If you're not sure someone is being honest, sometimes you can ask for proof.

I'm the fastest runner in our class.

Let's have a race and see.

Or talk about it with someone you trust.

Harry said I was stupid.

In America, we expect the truth from the people we elect to work for us and run the government. When leaders are honest with us, keep their word, and tell us what's really going on, only then can we trust them.

We will investigate the cause.

Use your own eyes and ears. And demand to know the truth.

Respect Free Speech

We all love having freedom. Doing what you want, not getting bossed around, being independent—even toddlers want that!

We have many freedoms in our country, but there is one that you probably count on every day: All citizens have a right to say what they believe. This is called freedom of speech.

Don't be scared to speak up and say what you mean.

If people don't listen, don't give up. Try again.

The goal in America is for everyone's voice to be heard. Part of the government's job is to protect your right to speak. But that doesn't guarantee it will happen for everyone. If you get to say what you believe, then so does everybody else. You may not even like what others have to say!

When there is freedom of speech, you can expect to have arguments.

That team stinks.

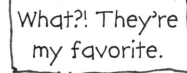

What?! They're my favorite.

How to Have an Argument

1. Listen. Don't interrupt.
2. Expect and ask others to listen to you.
3. Tell the truth.
4. Know what you are talking about.
5. You can still disagree.
6. Or maybe you can find a compromise.

In a compromise, each of you will give up something you want, to find a solution that both of you can accept.

The poster should be blue.

No, it should be red.

What if we used red and blue?

24

Free speech is so powerful that a kid citizen learns to use it carefully. Saying something just because you can isn't a good reason.

When kid citizens use their words thoughtfully and treat what others say with respect and consideration, we have what is called civility.

Having rules about how to be free may seem strange. Isn't freedom about *not* having rules? But our freedom can't exist without rules, compromise, and civility. It's like a seesaw, balancing between freedom and respect for rules.

Understand Democracy

Our country's government is called a democracy. That means it is supposed to be a government run by all the people. Our country didn't always work this way.

More than two hundred years ago, the people who created this government found the courage to stand up to the English king who ruled them. They wanted the freedom to govern themselves so much that they fought a war over it.

It took many years and many lives lost, but we won our independence.

Ever since, we have had the same goals for our democracy: to share rights equally, to make fair laws, to seek the truth, to defend our freedom, and to have our citizens vote for the country's leaders.

But the only way a democracy survives is when citizens care about and work together to reach these goals. And that includes you.

Stand Up for Democracy

Being free to speak what you believe is already powerful. Adding more voices increases your power to be heard.

As kid citizens, you and your friends can all help solve a problem. You don't have to work alone.

Kid citizens can work together to make things better for everyone.

When citizens organize in public to stand up peacefully for something they believe in, they are using another of our freedoms: the freedom of assembly.

You may be young today, but you and your friends will grow up and become the new voters and the new leaders. America needs you!

31

Words for Kid Citizens to Know

citizen: legal resident of a country who owes loyalty to the country and is owed all its protections

civility: acts that show others respect and consideration and help create cooperation in a society

compromise: when opposing sides give something up in order to reach an agreement

democracy: type of government where citizens choose by voting who will lead their country and how it should be governed

election: organized casting of votes in favor of or against certain decisions or candidates for a specific job

equality: being the same in size, value, number, power, or quality

government: system set up to protect and regulate people in a society

justice: fair treatment; using authority to maintain what is right

laws: rules a government makes to tell the people and the government what they can and cannot do

truth: what matches reality or the real state of things; what is honest and accurate

Speak truth to Power!

For Cora, Julian, and Leo—citizens in training

About This Book

The illustrations for this book were done in watercolors, permanent ink, gouache, and colored pencils on cold-press Bristol paper. This book was edited by Andrea Spooner and designed by Véronique Lefèvre Sweet. The production was supervised by Patricia Alvarado, and the production editor was Marisa Finkelstein. The text was set in Bodoni Book and Marc Brown's hand-lettered font, and the display type is Marc Brown's handwriting.

Little, Brown and Company • Hachette Book Group • 1290 Avenue of the Americas, New York, NY 10104 • Visit us at LBYR.com • First Edition: September 2020 • Little, Brown and Company is a division of Hachette Book Group, Inc. • The Little, Brown name and logo are trademarks of Hachette Book Group, Inc. • The publisher is not responsible for websites (or their content) that are not owned by the publisher. • Library of Congress Cataloging-in-Publication Data • Names: Brown, Laurene Krasny, author. | Brown, Marc Tolon, author. | Little, Brown and Company. • Title: Democracy for dinosaurs: a guide for young citizens / Laurie Krasny Brown, Marc Brown. • Description: New York: Little, Brown and Company, [2020] • Identifiers: LCCN 2019020131 | ISBN 9780316534529 (Hardcover) | Subjects: LCSH: Democracy—Juvenile literature. | Civics—Juvenile literature. | Dinosaurs—Juvenile literature. • Classification: LCC JC423 .B814 2020 | DDC 321.8—dc23 • LC record available at https://lccn.loc.gov/2019020131 • ISBN 978-0-316-53452-9 (hardcover) • PRINTED IN CHINA • APS •
10 9 8 7 6 5 4 3 2 1

A Word from the Author

Our democracy depends upon the informed participation of its citizens for its survival and success. First, citizens must learn the principles that lie at its foundation: individual freedom, truth, justice and the rule of law, equal rights, voting in fair elections, and advocacy for improvements in government. These values must be understood and embraced as essential and worth protecting. This book sets out to show children how these same ideals from their personal lives are also meant to guide how our government does its work.

The subject of democracy is rich and complex. A brief picture book cannot presume to capture a comprehensive discussion of all the key tenets in a democratic government. For example, I omitted freedom of the press, focusing instead on the arguably more relatable freedom of speech and the right to peacefully assemble. I also didn't identify the three branches of government and how they provide checks and balances in the distribution of power, since this book was organized around child-accessible values rather than government structure and functionality.

It is never too soon for children to practice putting democracy's core values to work. This book is a beginning step in children's civic education, an introduction to seeing themselves as citizens of their community and country.

To-Do List

The more you practice being a citizen, the better at it you will be. This is your country!

Plan elections at home and at school. Vote on a class pet or favorite subject, or what's for snack.

Write letters and send e-mails to let leaders know your opinions.

Listen to other people. Listening helps you understand what someone else thinks and why.

Ask questions about America. Find out about people who hurt it and who helped make it better, and learn from the helpers!